The Ultimate *Lion* Book for Kids

BELLANOVA
MELBOURNE · SOFIA · BERLIN

www.bellanovabooks.com

Copyright © 2026 by Jenny Kellett

All rights reserved. No part of this book may be reproduced in any form by any electronic or mechanical means including photocopying, recording, or information storage and retrieval without permission in writing from the author.

ISBN: 978-619-264-076-7
Imprint: Bellanova Books

CONTENTS

Introduction 4
Lion subspecies 6
    Asiatic lion 8
    African lion 10
Lion Facts 12
Lion Conservation 70
Lion Quiz 74
    Answers 79
Word search 80
    Solution 82
Sources 83
Also by Jenny Kellett 86

INTRODUCTION

Lions are the mightiest of the big cats, often called the **'king of beasts'**, and for good reason. With their majestic mane and powerful roar, lions have captured our imaginations for centuries.

But there are so many more reasons why lions are incredible animals that deserve our admiration and respect. From their incredible hunting skills and social behavior to their adaptations for survival in the wild, there's always something new and fascinating to learn about these magnificent creatures.

Get ready for a roar-some time as we head into the roar-tastic world of lions. *Let's go!*

LION SUBSPECIES

Did you know there are two types of lions? And here's another surprise: not all lions live in Africa!

The two lion subspecies are the **African lion and the Asiatic lion**.

Even though all lions are part of the same species, scientists split them into these two groups in 2017. Why? Because it helps researchers learn more about each group and figure out the best ways to protect them in the wild.

Now let's take a closer look at both types of lions—and see what makes each one special!

A male African lion.

ASIATIC LION
Panthera leo persica

The Asiatic lion, also known as the **Indian lion**, is a rare subspecies of lion that is found only in the Gir Forest in India.

There are less than 500 remaining in the wild, and they are listed as **Endangered** on the IUCN Red List of Threatened Species.

Asiatic lions are smaller than African lions, with males weighing up to around 440 pounds (200 kg) and females around 280 pounds (125 kg). They have a distinct fold of skin on their bellies, which other lion subspecies don't have. Asiatic lions

also have shorter and less dense manes than African lions. The mane of a male Asiatic lion is also usually darker than that of a male African lion.

Asiatic lions have also adapted to their unique habitat in the Gir Forest of India. For example, they have evolved to hunt smaller prey than African lions, such as deer and antelope. They are also able to survive in a drier, more arid environment than African lions, which allows them to go for longer periods without water.

AFRICAN LION
Panthera leo leo

African lions are found in sub-Saharan Africa. They are the more well-known of the two subspecies, as there are many more of them than Asiatic lions. African lions are known for their striking appearance. The males are famous for their big, beautiful manes.

African lions tend to be larger than Asiatic lions, with males weighing up to 550 pounds (250 kg).

Sadly, like Asiatic lions, African lions also face several threats that put their survival at risk. However, people are working hard to protect African lions. They are creating protected parks and nature reserves where lions can live safely, and teaching local people how to live together with lions.

LION FACTS

The average male lion weighs between 160-225 kg (350-496 lb), depending on where they are from. Southern African lions are the heaviest.

• • •

The average female lion weighs between 110-143 kg (240-316 lb).

• • •

The heaviest lion ever recorded weighed an incredible 375 kg (827 lb)!

Lions are the second-fastest land mammals in Africa — they can reach speeds of up to 81 km/h (50.3 mph), but only in very short bursts.

• • •

The roar of a lion can be heard 8 km (5 miles) away.

• • •

Lions roar mostly at nighttime, and they do it to let others know they are there.

• • •

Lions don't only roar. They make a range of noises, including purring, bleating, humming and puffing.

Two male lions in Tanzania.

Most wild lions can be found in southern and eastern Africa, however, their numbers are rapidly decreasing. In the late half of the 20th century, lion numbers decreased by an estimated 30-50%.

Researchers estimate there are 16,500 and 47,000 lions living in the wild in Africa today.

• • •

Unlike other cat species, lions are very sociable. They usually live in prides that include males, females and a few cubs.

• • •

Lions spend an average of two hours a day walking and 50 minutes eating.

• • •

Like domestic cats, lions spend a lot of time resting — up to 20 hours a day!

A young male lion. Can you see his mane starting to grow?
Credit: Frans Van Heerden

Young male lions often form "bachelor groups" after leaving their birth pride. They'll travel, hunt, and practice fighting together for a few years—almost like a lion teen squad—until they're strong enough to challenge older males and try to take over a pride.

Lions are most active just after dusk. This is when they usually do their hunting.

• • •

Most male lions have distinctive manes, while female lions do not.

• • •

There might not be any lions living in the wild in Europe, but many European countries have a lion as their national animal, including Bulgaria, Albania, England, Luxembourg, Belgium and the Netherlands.

In the wild, lions live for around 12–15 years. In captivity, they live for up to 20 years.

• • •

Evidence from cave paintings suggests that lions didn't always have a mane. In fact, the mane may have evolved 320,000–190,000 years ago.

• • •

Different species within the *Panthera* genus (which includes the other big cats) have been cross-bred to produce new breeds such as ligers, tigons, leopons and jaglions. Males from hybrid breeds are usually infertile.

White lions exist, but they are very rare. They have a genetic condition called **leucism**, which is different from albinism.

• • •

Lionesses are better hunters than lions, as they can run 30% faster. Male lions protect the pride while the lionesses are out hunting.

• • •

As lions can only run short distances quickly, they get as close as possible to their prey before attacking.

A lion in South Africa with his prey. *Credit: Frans Van Heerden*

Young lions don't start hunting until they are one year old, and it's not until they are two years old that they are good hunters.

• • •

Fossil records show that lions used to exist in Europe and even in Siberia, however, they became extinct due to global warming around 11,900 years ago.

• • •

Despite being called 'the king of the jungle', there are no lions living in jungles.

White lions (*above*) aren't a separate species—they're regular African lions with a rare genetic trait called leucism, which makes their fur very pale but doesn't turn their eyes pink like true albinos. They're most famous in the Timbavati region of South Africa, where white lions have been seen in the wild.

The darker a lion's mane, the older it is. A thick, dark mane is a good indication of a healthy lion.

• • •

Asiatic lions generally have sparser manes than their African relatives.

• • •

Most male West African lions in Pendjari National Park are either maneless or have very short manes.

• • •

The word 'Simba' means lion in Swahili. The word also means 'aggressive', 'king' and 'strong'.

Lions' heels don't touch the ground when they walk.

• • •

The word for lion in Turkish and Mongolian is 'Aslan'. This is also the name of the lion in C.S. Lewis's book *The Chronicles of Narnia*.

• • •

While they don't love water, lions are great swimmers when they need to cross water.

• • •

Wild lions eat between 4.5-11.3 kg (10-25 lbs) of meat a day. Male lions need more.

THE ULTIMATE LION BOOK FOR KIDS

Lions are the only cats that have a tuft on the end of their tails.

• • •

Sadly, only one in ten male lions make it to adulthood. The majority die after leaving their pride (the older males usually kick them out) at the age of two. Lionesses generally stay behind in the pride.

• • •

Lions have great night vision. They can see six times better in the dark than humans. Can you see the white patch under their eyes? This is used to reflect light into their eyes. They also have a reflective coating on the back of their eyes to capture maximum moonlight.

Lions mostly see in blues and greens.

• • •

The largest population of lions in Africa is in Tanzania.

• • •

Lionesses are pregnant with cubs for around 3.5 months. The typical number of cubs a lioness will have is 3, but it ranges from 1-6.

• • •

Lions come in all different colors, including red, yellow, tan and brown.

A male lion showing us his teeth.

Prides have an average of 13 members, but they can range from 2-40 lions.

• • •

Lions can't properly roar until the age of two.

• • •

Lions are **apex predators**, meaning that they are at the top of the food chain and have no natural predators.

Lions are also **keystone predators**. This means that they have a huge impact on their surrounding habitat. If lions were gone, the whole ecosystem would change. Other keystone predators around the world include wolves, sea otters and the jaguar.

...

Lions are mostly **diurnal** — much more so than other cats. This means that they are most active during the day and rest mostly at night. However, they will hunt on bright nights if they are hungry.

A lion and a cub in a zoo in Poland.

A wild male lion in Masai Mara National Reserve, Kenya.

The small population of Asiatic lions living in western India are critically endangered.

• • •

The main cause for the decline in lions is habitat loss.

• • •

Carvings and paintings of lions dating back 17,000 years were found in caves in France.

• • •

There are two subspecies of lion recognised by the **Cat Classification Task Force**: *Panthera leo leo* and *Panthera leo melanochaita*.

The *Panthera leo leo* subspecies includes the Asiatic lion, the extinct Barbary lion and lion populations in the north and western parts of Africa.

• • •

The *Panthera leo melanochaita* subspecies includes East and Southern Africa lions, as well as the extinct Cape lion.

• • •

The tuft on the end of a lion's tail doesn't develop until it is around 5 ½ months of age. By seven months, it should be fully visible.

An Asiatic lion cub in Gir National Park, India. *Credit: Vicky Chauhan.*

A male lion cub's mane starts growing when it is around one year old.

• • •

Although a dark mane can mean a lion is stronger and more fertile, they can also really suffer in the hot heat!

• • •

You will never find a lion in a rainforest, and they always try to avoid any type of closed forests. They prefer open savannahs and grassy plains.

• • •

Groups of male lions are called **coalitions**.

African lions enjoy finding shade under acacia trees. Acacia trees are also a favorite food of giraffes, one of the lions favorite meals!

• • •

Lionesses may sometimes leave their pride and become nomadic.

• • •

Lionesses don't tolerate any outside females entering their pride. New females can only enter a pride if there is a death or birth.

An African lion in Kruger National Park, South Africa.

Nomadic lions can be alone or in pairs. They may also decide to join or rejoin a pride, although this is usually after several years of being nomadic.

• • •

The area where a pride roams is called a "**pride area**", while the area where nomadic lions roam is called a "**range**".

• • •

Asiatic lions are more likely to roam alone. Male and female Asiatic lions will only associate with one another if they are mating.

Lions mostly eat mammals, weighing between 190–550 kg (420–1,210 lb).

• • •

African lions' favorite meals include blue wildebeest, zebra, giraffe, African buffalo and gemsbok.

• • •

In Asia, lions prefer to eat sambar deer and chital. They may also prey on domestic livestock such as cows.

• • •

Lions may sometimes kill other predators such as cheetahs, leopards and hyenas, but they will rarely eat them.

A male Asiatic lion marking his territory.
Credit: Sumeet Moghe

THE ULTIMATE LION BOOK FOR KIDS

An Asiatic lioness. Credit: Sumeet Moghe

After a kill, lions will usually eat their prey in the same spot. Sometimes, though, they drag it off to a more secret location.

• • •

If food is scarce, lions will often scavenge on already dead animals. They look out for vultures circling in the sky to tell them where to find the food.

• • •

Lions and hyenas compete for almost all of the same food. Lions will often steal kills from hyenas!

In some parts of Africa, around 71% of hyena deaths can be attributed to lions. When lion populations in Masai Mara National Park declined, hyena numbers drastically increased.

• • •

After a lioness gives birth, she will usually wait 6-8 weeks before going back into the pride with her cubs.

• • •

Although adult lions don't have any natural predators, they can often be killed by attacks from other lions, or from humans.

An African lion in Serengeti, Tanzania

Lions will often use head rubbing, nuzzling and licking to communicate with other lions. Nuzzling is believed to be a type of friendly greeting.

• • •

There are many large, protected areas in Africa where lions can live relatively safe from humans.

• • •

In Gir National Park, the only place where Asiatic lions still exist, conservationists have successfully helped increase lion numbers from 180 in 1974 to over 400.

Around the world, there are over 1,000 African lions and 100 Asiatic lions in zoos.

• • •

While most lions don't seek out humans to eat, there are cases where male lions have done so. In 1898, 28 railway workers in Kenya were taken by lions. Lions generally only eat humans if they have no other food source.

• • •

In much African folklore, the lion is described as being stupid and easily tricked by other animals.

A young lion in Tsavo West National Park, Mangani, Kenya.

Lions feature in many of the world's most popular movies including *The Lion King*, *The Wizard of Oz* and *Madagascar*. Which is your favorite?

• • •

Leo the Lion is one of the most famous Hollywood lions of all time. You might recognize his roar from the beginning of MGM movies. He has also featured in many advertisements and commercials.

• • •

One of the sky's most famous constellations is Leo, which is in the Northern Hemisphere. Leo is also a zodiac sign.

If you were born between July 23 and August 22 your zodiac sign is Leo.

• • •

Lions are the only big cats in which the male looks different from the female.

• • •

In 2002 a lioness adopted an abandoned baby antelope. This was something scientists had never seen before!

• • •

Lions have the weakest bite of all big cats, however, it's still 30 times stronger than a domestic cat's! Jaguars have the strongest bite of all the big cats.

Lions may be renowned as 'man-eaters', but the deadliest land animal is the hippopotamus! They kill around 500 humans per year, compared to around 100 that are killed by lions.

• • •

Lionesses often bring back small animals, such as baby antelope, still alive to help their cubs practice their hunting skills.

• • •

Lions can't move their eyes side-to-side very well, so they have to move their whole heads to look around.

A lion's tongue is so rough it can peel the skin off of its prey with a few licks.

• • •

African lions have loose skin on their bellies, which means they have less chance of being injured if they are kicked.

• • •

Lions have a scent gland between their toes. When they scratch on trees, this is another way of marking their territory.

At the bottom of each lion's whisker is a black spot. The patterns these make are completely unique, so biologists can identify different lions — kind of like a human fingerprint!

• • •

Lions have moveable ears, which can adjust to the direction of the sound. This combined with their amazing hearing means they can hear prey up to 1.6 km (1 mile) away.

• • •

The famous Great Sphinx in Egypt has the body of a lion.

In Botswana, around 90 percent of lions are infected with FIV, which is the feline equivalent of HIV. Most house cats are (or should be) vaccinated against this disease.

• • •

Bulgaria's currency is the leva, which means 'lion' in old Bulgarian.

• • •

Lions are mentioned several times in the Bible, including in the Book of Daniel.

Lion claws are 7.6 cm (3 in) long — about the length of a human finger.

World Lion Day is celebrated on August 10. On this day, conservationists and lion enthusiasts like yourself help to spread awareness about the declining lion populations.

When lion cubs are born they have light black spots on their fur, which eventually disappear as they grow up.

Just like domestic cats, lionesses will carry their young cubs around in their mouths. They grab them by the scruff of their neck, which causes them to go limp — it doesn't hurt at all!

• • •

Lion cubs weigh just 1.5 kg (3.3 lbs) when they are born.

• • •

If you want to help save lions, there are many ways that you can contribute! Many charities and organizations such as the *Big Cat Initiative* from National Geographic, allow you to donate money or even adopt a lion. We take a closer look in the next chapter.

LION CONSERVATION

Lions are majestic creatures that are loved and admired by people all around the world. Unfortunately, lions are facing many threats, such as habitat loss, human-wildlife conflict, and poaching. This is why lion conservation is important to help protect these incredible animals.

There are many organizations and individuals working hard to protect lions and their habitats. One way they do this is by working with local communities to reduce conflict between people and lions. This can involve things like building fences to keep lions away from livestock or providing farmers with alternative sources of income so they don't have to rely on their livestock for a living.

Another important part of lion conservation is protecting their habitats. This can involve things like creating national parks or protected areas where lions can live without interference from humans. It can also involve working to reduce deforestation and other activities that are destroying lion habitats.

Finally, lion conservation also involves efforts to stop poaching. Poaching is the illegal hunting of animals for their body parts, such as lion skins and bones. This is a serious problem for lions, and efforts are being made to stop poaching and to prosecute those who engage in it.

By working together to protect lions and their habitats, we can help ensure that these amazing animals continue to thrive for generations to come. If you love lions, you can help by learning more about them and supporting organizations that work to protect them.

HOW CAN YOU HELP LIONS?

Spread the word: Talk to your friends and family about lions and how important it is to protect them. You can share fun facts about lions and the threats they face.

Donate to lion charities: Instead of getting gifts on your birthday, consider asking your friends and family to donate to a lion charity, such as the *African Wildlife Foundation* or *Panthera*.

Support ecotourism: When you go on vacation, consider visiting national parks and wildlife reserves that support animal conservation. This can help provide economic benefits to local communities and protect animals' habitats.

Reduce your ecological footprint: Simple actions like turning off lights when you leave a room or using reusable water bottles can help reduce your ecological footprint and protect the planet.

LION QUIZ

Now test your knowledge in our Lion Quiz! Answers are on page 79.

1 What do you call a group of lions?

2 Lions are the biggest type of cat. True or false?

3 How many hours a day do lions spend sleeping?

4 When are lions most active?

5 When do lion cubs start hunting?

6 Lions live in jungles. True or false?

7 What is the Swahili name for a lion?

A lioness protecting her cubs.

8 What do lions have that no other cats have?

9 Lions purr. True or false?

10 In which country is the largest population of lions?

11 There are two species of lion. Can you name them?

12 Can you name some of a lion's favorite foods?

13 Where do lions prefer to eat their prey?

14 How long does a lioness wait before introducing her cubs to her pride?

15 In which national park in India can you find Asiatic lions?

16 Lions have great hearing. True or false?

17 How much does a cub weigh when it's born?

18 At what age can lions start to roar?

19 How can you tell a male lions age?

20 When is World Lion Day celebrated?

ANSWERS

1. A pride.
2. False. Tigers are the largest.
3. Around 20 hours.
4. After dusk.
5. One year old.
6. False.
7. Simba.
8. A tuft on their tail.
9. False.
10. Tanzania.
11. Asiatic and African.
12. Blue wildebeest, zebra, giraffe, African buffalo and gemsbok.
13. In the spot they killed it. However, they will sometimes drag it to a safer place.
14. 6-8 weeks.
15. Gir National Park.
16. True.
17. Around 1.5kg (3.3lbs).
18. Two years old.
19. The darker his mane, the older he is.
20. August 10.

LION WORD SEARCH

```
F D S N J F D S X P C V
Y N B L X F D A W R N A
T Y T R I Z X C V I E S
R Q W G J O V N H D A I
W S A V A N N A H E H A
D B G F C D S E P U T T
F Q W X R V C X S Z E I
G C Q W S I M B A S N C
H Y U Q H C C P O U F G
K T W B F R O A R N H F
N R W E V C X Z N M J H
V M A N E Q W E F G J L
```

CAN YOU FIND ALL THE WORDS BELOW IN THE WORD SEARCH PUZZLE ON THE LEFT?

LIONESS	ASIATIC	MANE
CUB	AFRICAN	PRIDE
SAVANNAH	ROAR	SIMBA

THE ULTIMATE LION BOOK FOR KIDS

SOLUTION

								P		
			L					R		A
			I					I		S
					O			D		I
	S	A	V	A	N	N	A	H	E	
		F				E				A
			R				S			T
	C			S	I	M	B	A	S		I
			U			C				C
			B		R	O	A	R		
								N		
	M	A	N	E						

SOURCES

"91 Roaring Lion Facts You Won't Believe | Fact Retriever". 2020. Factretriever.Com.

"Lion Cubs - All The Important Facts You Should Know". 2020. Wildlife Detective.

"Fun Lion Facts For Kids - Interesting Facts About Lions, Pride, Mane, Lioness". 2020. Sciencekids.Co.Nz.

"Lioness Adopts Third Baby Antelope." BBC News. April 1, 2002. Accessed: October 19, 2020

"Local Currency in Bulgaria." Currencyname. 2015. Accessed: October 20, 2020.

Thompson, Helen. **"Yes, Lions Will Hunt Humans if Given the Chance."** June 5, 2015. Accessed: October 18, 2020

Welsbacher, Anne. **Lions (Wild Cats).** Edina, MN: Abdo Publishing Company, 2000.

***Blewett, Ashley with Daniel Raven-Ellison.*
Mission: Lion Rescue.** Washington D.C.: National Geographic Society, 2014.

"Lion". 2020. En.Wikipedia.Org. https://en.wikipedia.org/wiki/Lion. Accessed: 19 October 2020.

"10 Roarsome Lion Facts! | National Geographic Kids". 2019. National Geographic Kids. Accessed 19 October 2020.

"Ten Interesting Facts About Lions | Blog Posts | WWF". 2020. World Wildlife Fund. Accessed 19 October 2020.

"Lion | Characteristics, Habitat, & Facts". 2020. Encyclopedia Britannica. Accessed 19 October 2020.

"African Lion – Fun Facts & Information For Kids". 2017. Folly Farm. Accessed 19 October 2020.

Rooooar!

We hope you loved exploring the world of lions! If this book made you smile, taught you something new, or made you say "Whoa!", please consider leaving a review where you bought it.

Reviews help other families find the book — and they help us keep making more awesome animal adventures.

Thank you for reading!

ALSO BY JENNY KELLETT

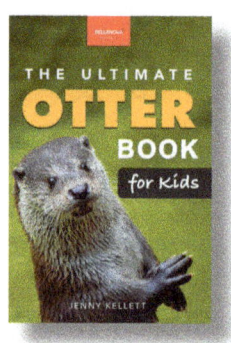  

... and more!

Available at

www.bellanovabooks.com

and all major online bookstores.